Colouring Love

A COLLECTION OF HAND DRAWN
LOVE FILLED MANDALAS

Love is the greatest healer

Pursue life with loving intention

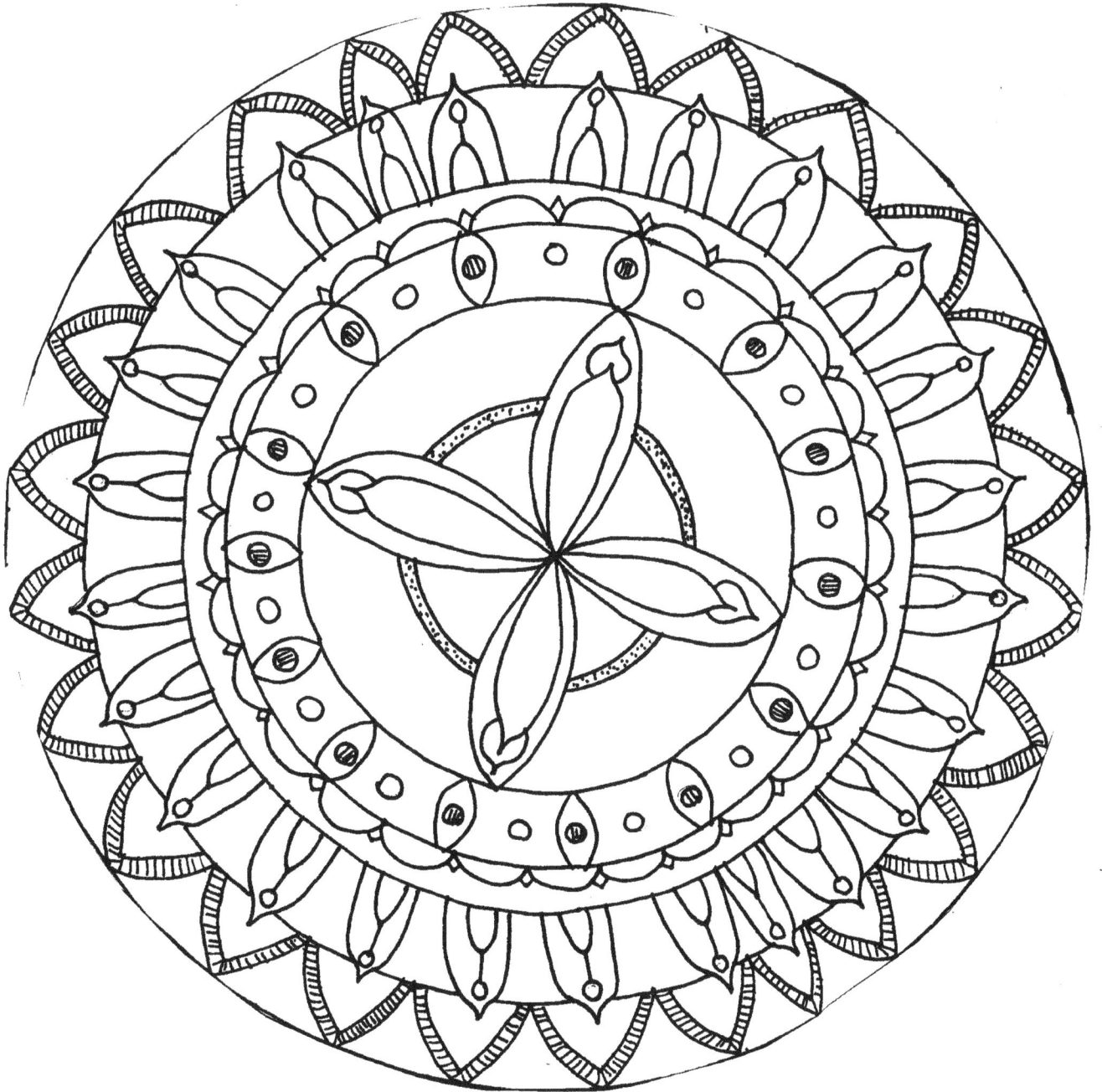

Loves helps
everything
grow
beautifully

Love
Conquers
All

Love
is
Love

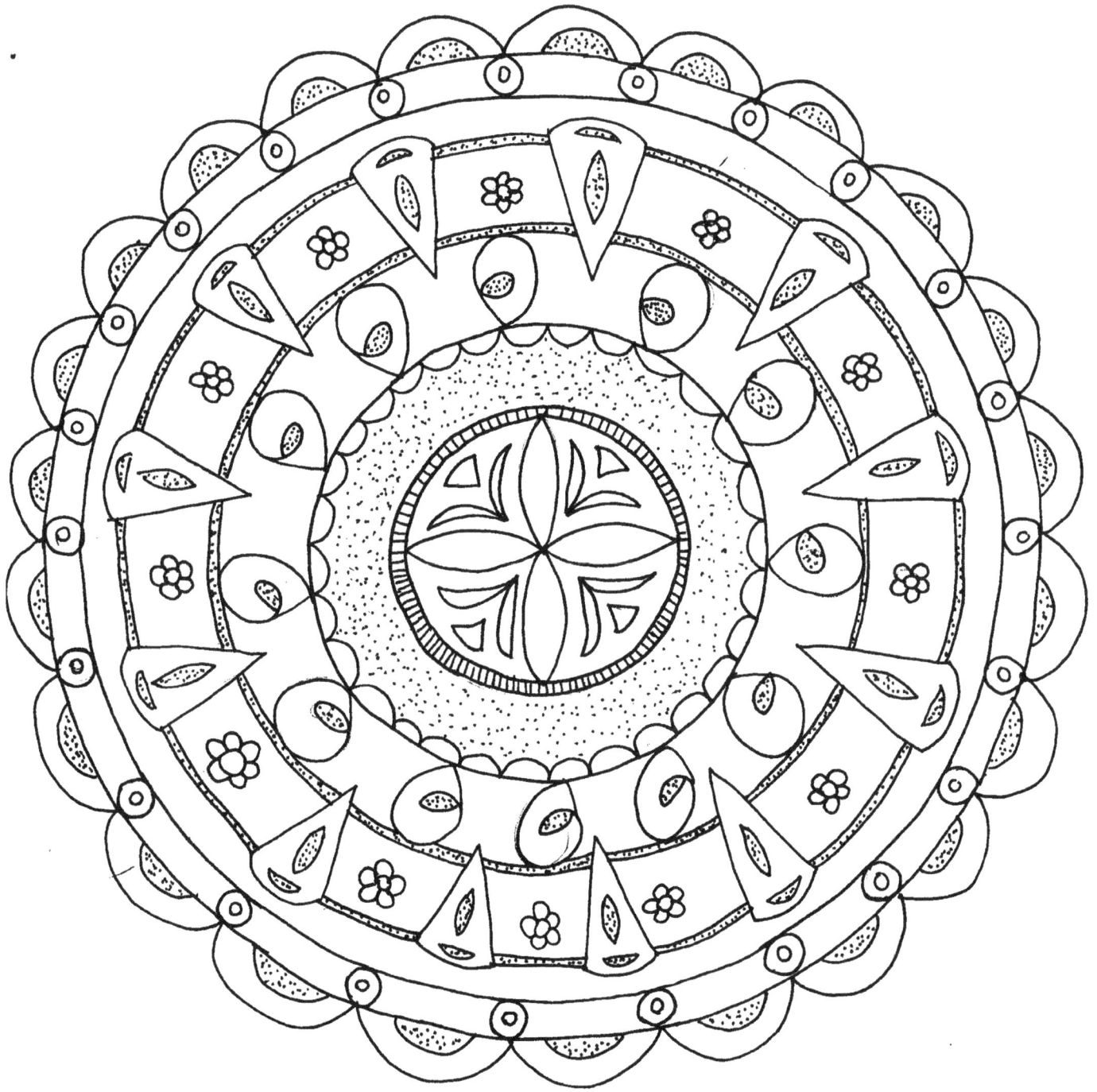

Love,
Joy
and
happiness

Love life and it will love you back

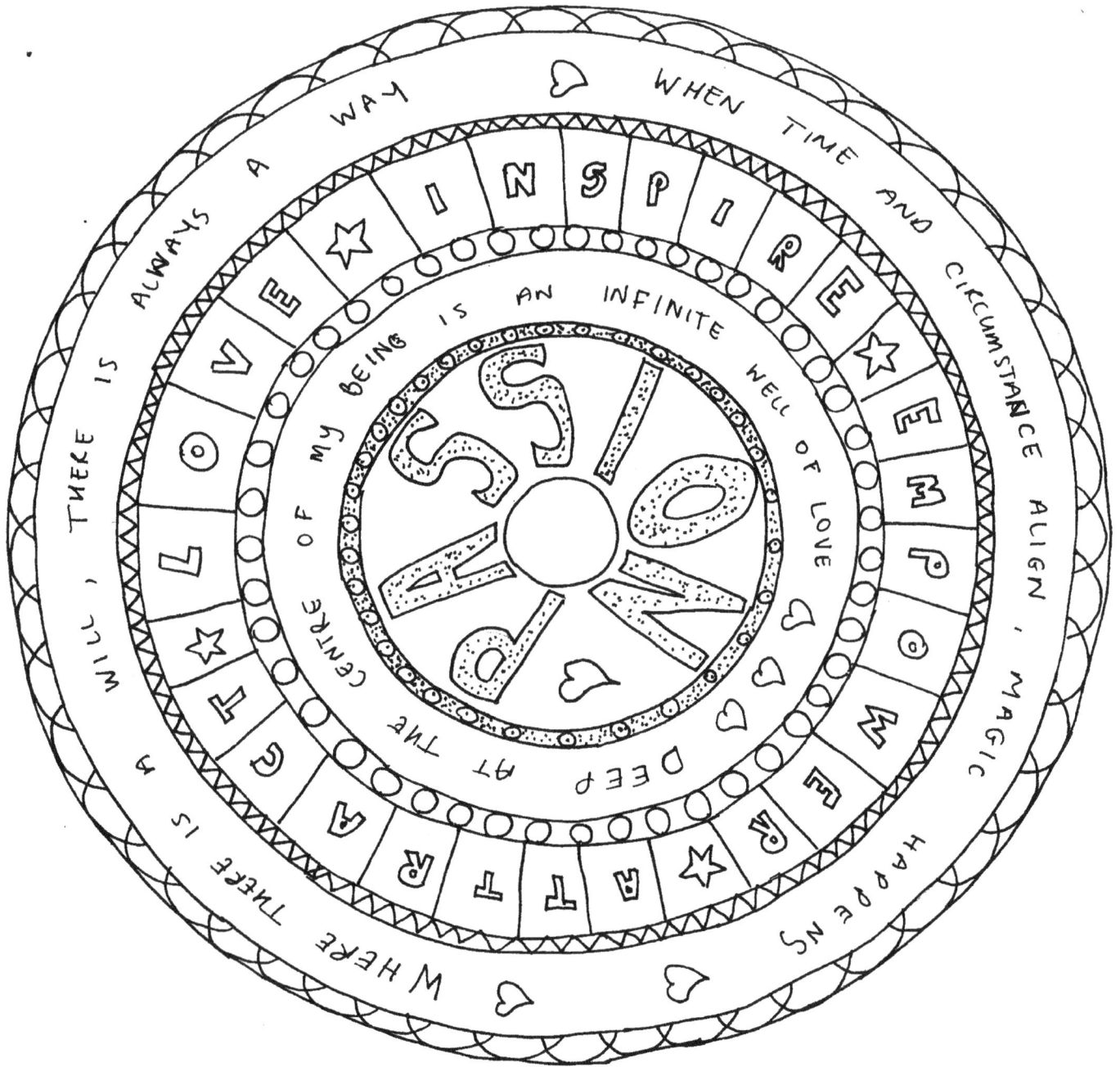

PASSION

INSPIRE EMPOWER ATTRACT LOVE

THERE IS ALWAYS A WAY WHEN TIME AND CIRCUMSTANCE ALIGN, MAGIC HAPPENS WHERE THERE IS A WILL,

OF MY BEING IS AN INFINITE WELL OF LOVE DEEP AT THE CENTRE

Be grateful
for the love
you receive

Deep at the centre of our being is an infinite well of love

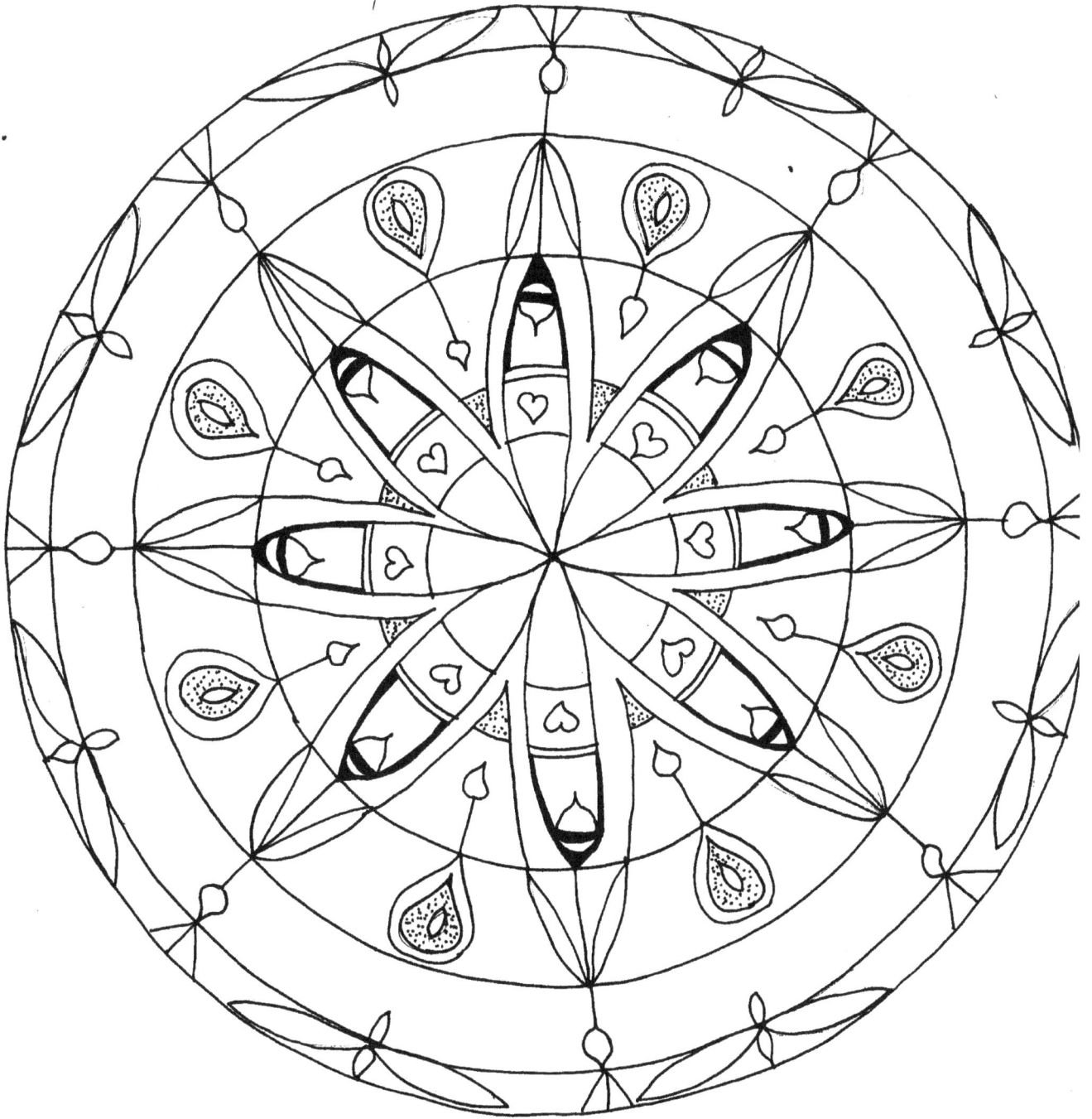

Fall in love with your life

LIVE

LAUGH

LOVE

Love is not
what you say,
it is what
you do

Design a
life you
love

Love is authentic, like a snowflake

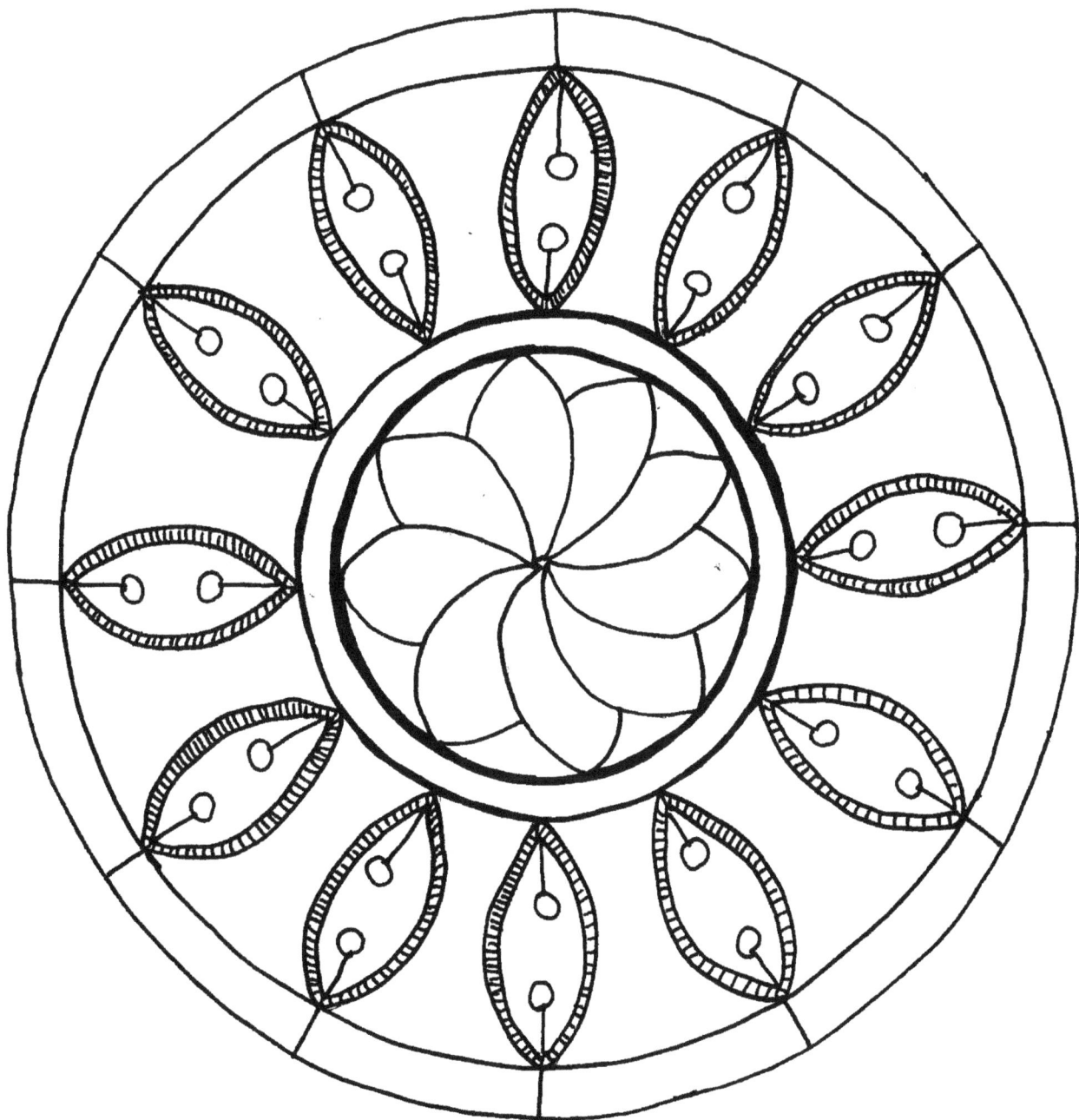

*Love is
a gift
to treasure*

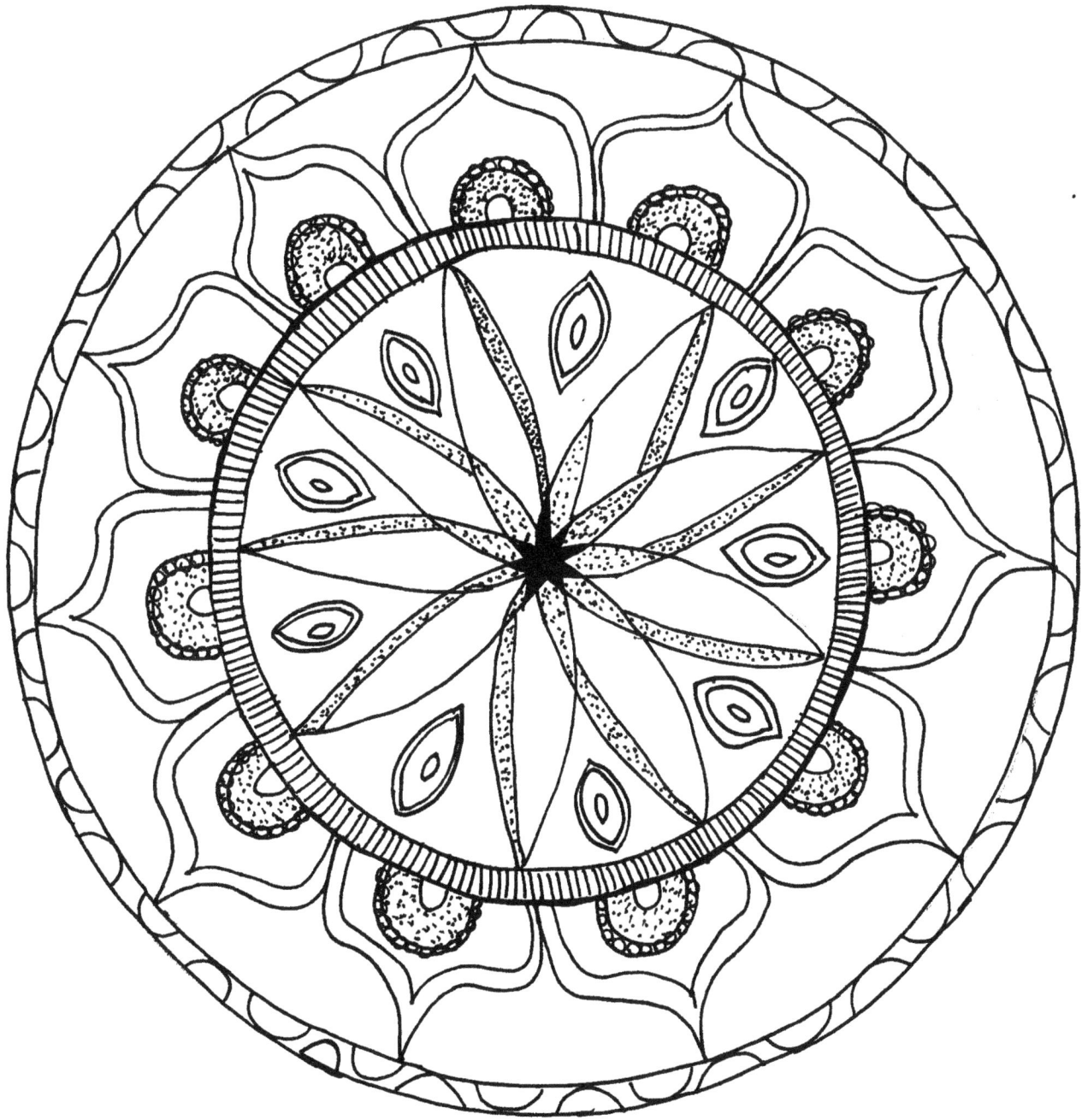

Loving energy
can overcome
any barrier

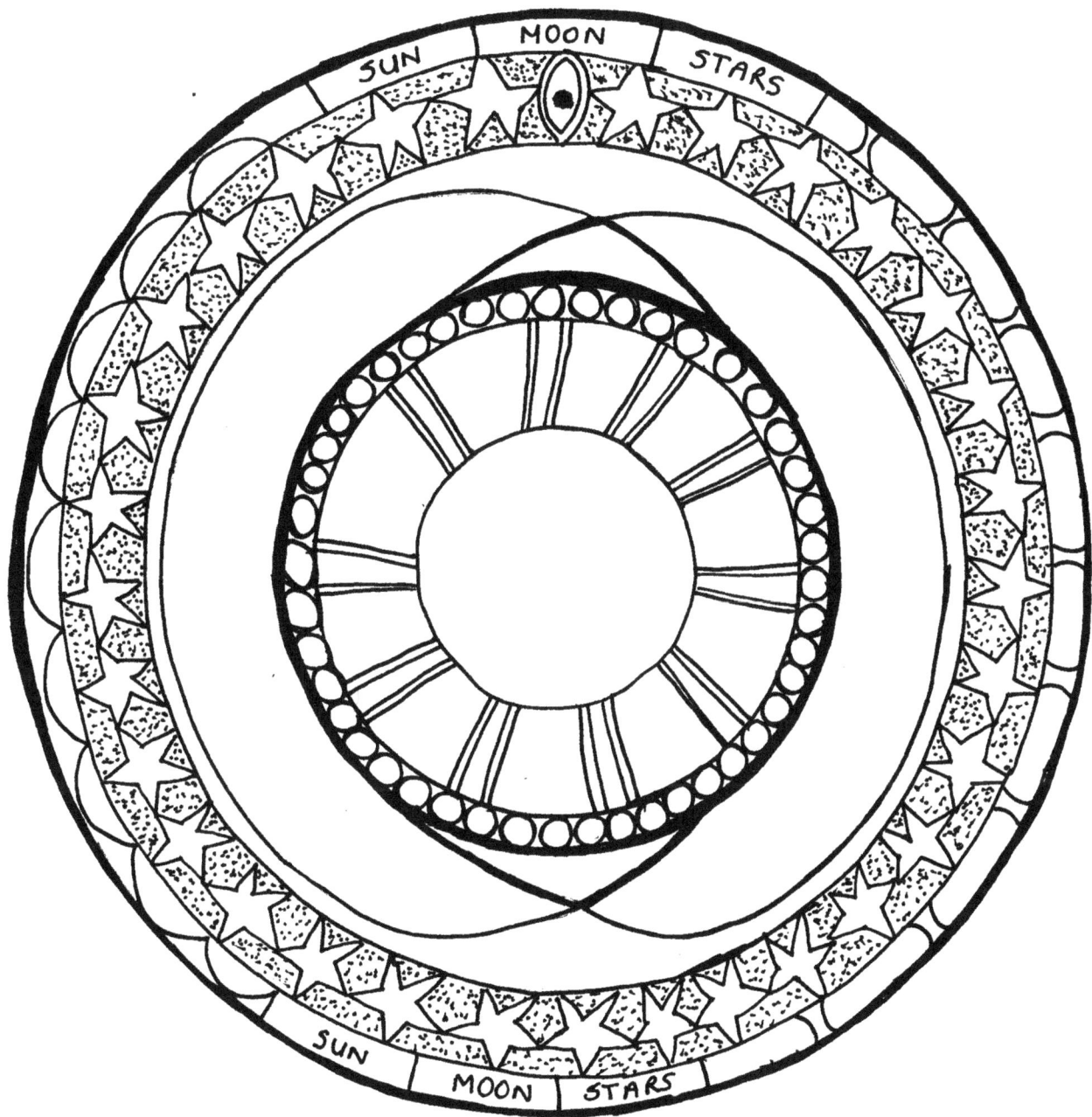

Love blossoms
when we
nuture it

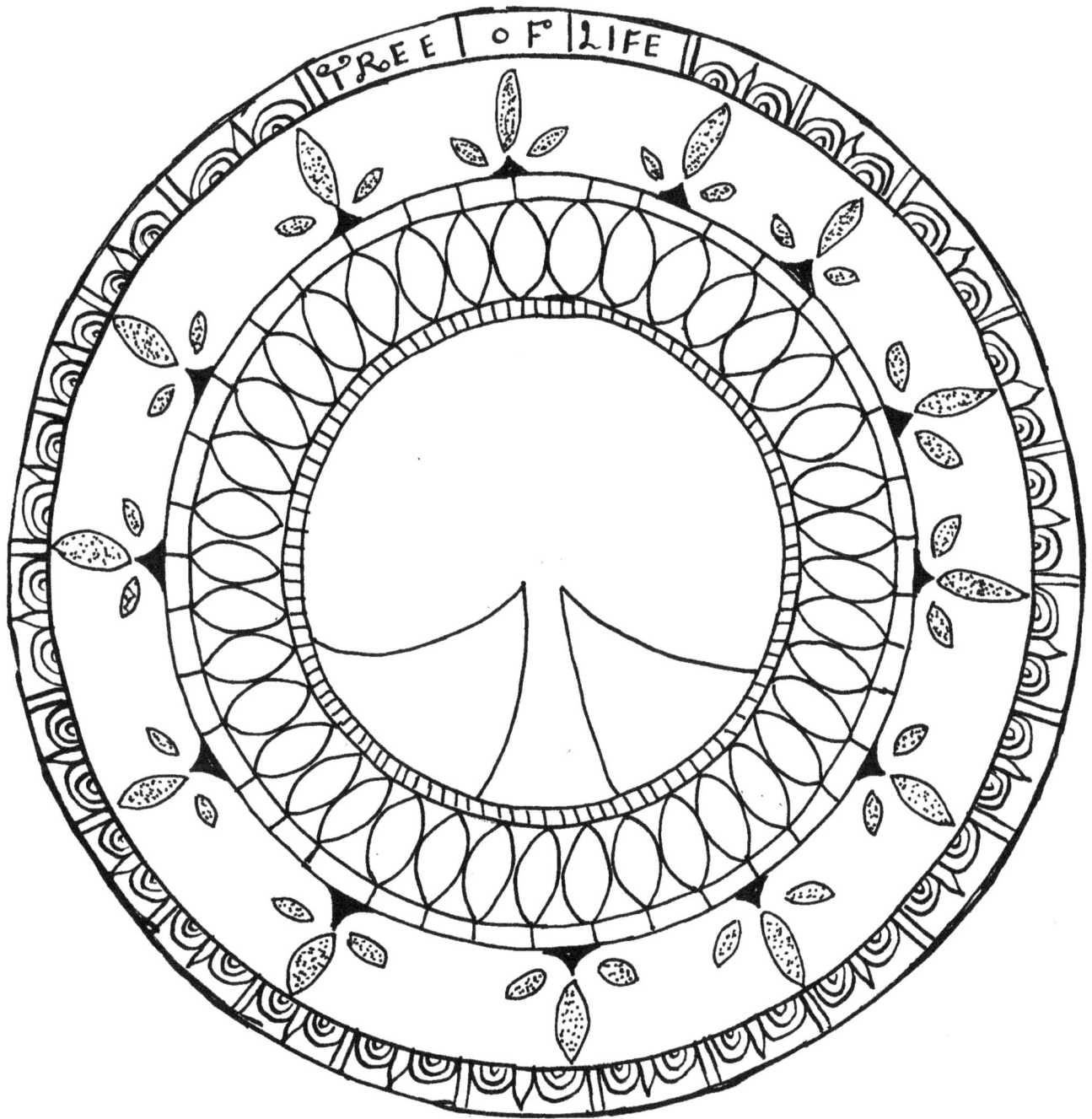

TREE OF LIFE

Draw your own mandala.

10 top tips to guide you.

1. Draw a circle on the page.
2. Begin drawing in the middle of the circle and work your way out. (maybe draw smaller circles at intervals within the bigger one)
3. Draw lightly in pencil first the design you would like.
4. Allow yourself to be open to inspiration and experimentation. This way you may channel some beautiful and unique work.
5. Look at other mandalas that you like for inspiration and incorporate your own twist on it. No two mandalas should be the same, think of them as a snowflake, each unique.
6. If you make a mistake you do not need to throw it out, try to work it out in the design. Add something new to enhance it.
7. You can add as many or as few elements as you like.
8. Love your work and it will show in the design.
9. Use a fine liner pen to go over your design and rub out the pencil.
10. Print yourself out a copy to colour in. This is your design, enjoy it!

www.ingramcontent.com/pod-product-compliance
Lightning Source LLC
Chambersburg PA
CBHW062006090426

42811CB00005B/770